The Blue Day Book

The Blue Day Book

A Lesson in Cheering Yourself Up

Bradley Trevor Greive

**Andrews McMeel
Publishing**

Kansas City

08 TWP 10 9 8 7 6 5

ISBN 13: 978-0-7407-4750-2
ISBN 10: 0-7407-4750-9

Library of Congress Control Number: 99-68167

Book design by Holly Camerlinck

To my wonderful parents, Fay and Trevor Greive,
who never stopped taking me out to see the world
even after I was bitten by penguins, twice.

Acknowledgments

There are so many incredible photographs in *The Blue Day Book* that it's not possible to credit every single photographer in the space we have. But I would like to say that the magic in every image speaks of a talent and purpose that my clumsy prose could only diminish. What wonderful breed of artist could squeeze so much into a fraction of a fraction of a moment? Thank you.

A tiny book like this appears deceptively simple. It is not. I owe great thanks to the many people who encouraged me to pursue the project, particularly after the first five rejections. My adorable sisters, Linley and Vanessa, led the charge along with my dear friends Basquali Skamaachi, Siimon Reynolds, Imogen Banks, and Jane Malone. Special awards are due to Sue Greaves, Emma McClure, and Norma Scott, who let me invade their photo archives without flinching, and of course to my editor, Christine Schillig, and her team at Andrews McMeel, who turned a scribbly submission into this beautiful little book.

I am particularly grateful to Al Zuckerman, my agent at Writers House in New York, and his faithful and witty assistant, Fay Greenfield, for setting me loose in America. I also want to say a special thank-you to marketing superstar Leslie Ferraro, who personally made up about one million photocopied submissions late one San Francisco summer night so that an impoverished Australian artist could have a shot at the big league. With friends like these I cannot fail.

The Blue Day Book

Everybody has blue days.

These are miserable days when you feel lousy,

grumpy,

lonely,

and utterly exhausted.

Days when you feel small and insignificant,

when everything seems just out of reach.

You can't rise to the occasion.

Just getting started seems impossible.

On blue days you can become paranoid
that everyone is out to get you.
(This is not always such a bad thing.)

You feel frustrated and anxious,

which can induce a nail-biting frenzy

that can escalate into a triple-chocolate-mud-cake-
eating frenzy in the blink of an eye!

13

On blue days you feel like you're floating
in an ocean of sadness.

You're about to burst into tears at any moment
and you don't even know why.

Ultimately, you feel like you're wandering
through life without purpose.

You're not sure how much longer
you can hang on,

and you feel like shouting,
'Will someone please shoot me!'

It doesn't take much to bring on a blue day.

You might just wake up
not feeling or looking your best,

find some new wrinkles,

put on a little weight,

or get a huge pimple on your nose.

You could forget your date's name

or have an embarrassing photograph published.

You might get dumped, divorced, or fired,

make a fool of yourself in public,

be afflicted with a demeaning nickname,

or just have a plain old bad-hair day.

Maybe work is a pain in the bum.

You're under serious pressure
to fill someone else's shoes,

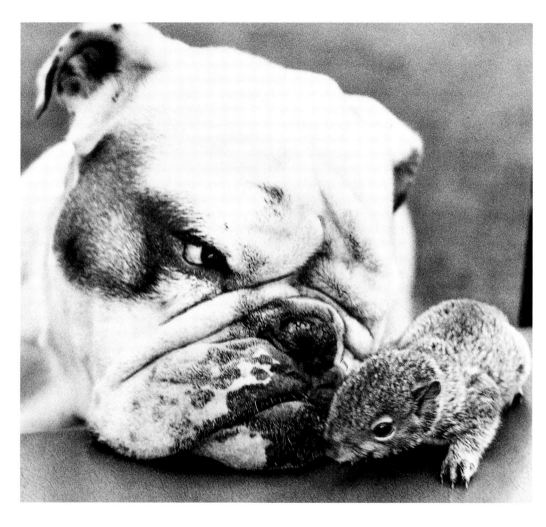

your boss is picking on you,

and everyone in the office
is driving you mad.

You might have a splitting headache,

or a slipped disk,

bad breath,

a toothache,

chronic gas,

dry lips,

or a nasty ingrown toenail.

Whatever the reason, you're convinced
that someone up there doesn't like you.

Oh, what to do, what to dooo?

Well, if you're like most people, you'll hide behind a
flimsy belief that everything will sort itself out. 43

Then you'll spend the rest of your life
looking over your shoulder, waiting for everything
to go wrong all over again.

All the while becoming crusty and cynical

or a pathetic, snivelling victim,

until you get so depressed that you lie down
and beg the earth to swallow you up

or, even worse, become addicted
to Billy Joel songs.

This is crazy, because you're only young once

and you're never old twice.

Who knows what fantastic things are in store
just around the corner?

After all, the world is full
of amazing discoveries,

things you can't even imagine right now.

There are delicious, happy sniffs,

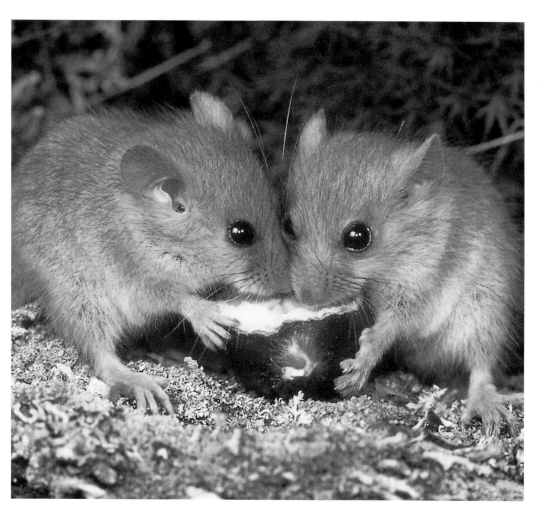

and scrumptious snacks to share. 55

Hey, you might end up fabulously rich

or even become a huge superstar (one day).

Sounds good, doesn't it?

But wait, there's more!

There are handstands,

and games to play,

and yoga

and karaoke

and wild, crazy, bohemian dancing.

But, best of all, there's romance.

Which means long dreamy stares,

whispering sweet nothings,

cuddles,

smooches,

more smooches,

and even more smooches,

a frisky love bite or two,

and then, well, anything goes.

So how can you find that blissful
'just sliding into a hot bubble bath'
kind of feeling?

It's easy.

First, stop slinking away from all those nagging issues.
It's time to face the music.

Now, just relax. Take some deep breaths
(in through the nose and out through the mouth).
Try to meditate if you can.

Or go for a walk to clear your head.

Accept the fact that you'll have to let go
of some emotional baggage.

Try seeing things from a different perspective.

Maybe you're actually the one at fault.
If that's the case, be big enough to say you're sorry
(it's never too late to do this).

If someone else is doing the wrong thing,
stand up tall and say, 'That's not right and I won't
stand for it!' It's okay to be forceful.

(It's rarely okay to blow raspberries.)

Be proud of who you are,

but don't lose the ability to laugh at yourself.

(This is a lot easier when you associate
with positive people.)

Live every day as if it were your last,
because one day it will be.

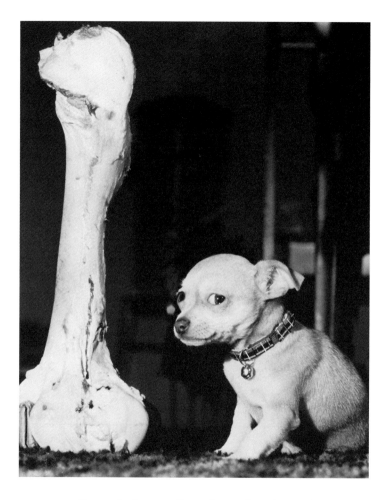

Don't be afraid to bite off
more than you can chew.

Take big risks.

Never hang back. Get out there and go for it.

After all, isn't that what life is all about?

I think so too.

Credits

Austral International
www.australphoto.com.au

Australian Picture Library
www.australianpicturelibrary.com.au

Getty Images
www.gettyimages.com

Photolibrary.com
www.photolibrary.com

D. Robert Franz
www.franzfoto.com

Detailed page credits for the remarkable photographers whose work appears in *The Blue Day Book* and other books by Bradley Trevor Greive are freely available at www.btgstudios.com.